Start Earning from Your Online Business

Valuable Information on How the Internet Can Change Your Financial Status

By: Karen Turner

9781635014976

Publishers Notes

Disclaimer – Speedy Publishing LLC

This publication is intended to provide helpful and informative material. It is not intended to diagnose, treat, cure, or prevent any health problem or condition, nor is intended to replace the advice of a physician. No action should be taken solely on the contents of this book. Always consult your physician or qualified health-care professional on any matters regarding your health and before adopting any suggestions in this book or drawing inferences from it.

The author and publisher specifically disclaim all responsibility for any liability, loss or risk, personal or otherwise, which is incurred as a consequence, directly or indirectly, from the use or application of any contents of this book.

Any and all product names referenced within this book are the trademarks of their respective owners. None of these owners have sponsored, authorized, endorsed, or approved this book.

Always read all information provided by the manufacturers' product labels before using their products. The author and publisher are not responsible for claims made by manufacturers.

This book was originally printed before 2014. This is an adapted reprint by Speedy Publishing LLC with newly updated content designed to help readers with much more accurate and timely information and data.

Speedy Publishing LLC

40 E Main Street, Newark, Delaware, 19711

Contact Us: 1-888-248-4521

Website: http://www.speedypublishing.co

REPRINTED Paperback Edition: 9781635014976:

Manufactured in the United States of America

DEDICATION

This book is dedicated to my family and friends. You have always been my support group. Thank you for constantly believing in me.

TABLE OF CONTENTS

CHAPTER 1- : WHY THE INTERNET IS THE MOST LUCRATIVE BUSINESS PLATFORM TODAY

As you read these words, there are millions of people making a full time income on the internet, working part time hours from the comfort of their own home. These people set their own working hours, live where ever they choose and have a ton of spare time to spend with their family, friends and simply do things they love to do. Does this sound like something you would like to be doing? Of course it is, why else would you have bought this guide! Well rest assured you have made the right decision by buying this guide. Because you are about to learn everything you need to know to get started on your internet business and be pointed in the right direction towards online business success. In this guide, you will not only learn the basics of starting an internet business. But learn of the many different online business models you can choose, and even analyze over 50 successful online businesses you can imitate! But before we get started, just so you are as existed as I am about doing business online. Here are some of the main reasons most people decide to start an online business:

• It takes very little money to start

Unlike a business in the "real world", an online business does not need a lot of startup money. All you need as an idea, a domain name, internet access and hosting...all of which can be had for under $100!

• You choose when you work

Who says you must work from 9 to 5 everyday? People who are NOT Internet Business owners! The Internet Business is the biggest proof why the statement "working from 9 to 5" is no longer true. With an Internet Business, you don't have to wake up in the wee hours of the morning so that you can get to work by 9am, anymore. You can start work at any time since you are your own boss!

• Work from the comfort of your own home

Where you put your computer is where you will be working! And since you're going to be working from home, you'll be saving at least two hours of your time each day by not having to travel to and from your work place during rush hours when everybody else is going to work or heading for home. That means you'll be saving at least 730 hours a year! Wouldn't you shudder at the thought of wasting 730 hours a year doing nothing productive?

Karen Turner

• With the internet, the whole world is your market!

By sitting in front of the computer, everyone in the world is now within your three feet. You leverage on free or low-cost software and hardware and the Internet Infrastructure, all of which when combined will give you leveraging power that far exceeds any conventional business, allowing you to achieve more and more with less and less work!

• You can fully automate your online business

If properly set up, some Internet Business models can be fully automated

• No need to work 8 hours a day every single day

Once you can automate your Internet Business in some way, you can use the time you saved to start another Internet Business, improve your existing business, or spend anyhow you like. You just spend the time online checking your mail religiously, promoting and expanding your business – all in front of your computer. And there is absolutely no need to spend even more than four hours online.

• Spend more time with family and friends

Owning an Internet Business gives you the privilege to have more time to spend with your family, or watch your children grow up. This is what most busy parents crave for. If you are one of them, then you will do well to seriously consider starting an Internet Business.

• Your online business can be all about your hobbies and passions

Now, this is my favorite reason for anybody wanting to start an Internet Business! The Internet Business allows your passion and dream to come to life, which is also the most important component of businesses of any kind.

• Online businesses have very little expenses

Believe it or not, some Internet Businesses can be set up and running at zero cost, if not very low. Other Internet Businesses can run with monthly operational expenses so low that they are negligible! So, you can rest assured you won't find me recommending products or services that cost thousands of dollars, the amount of money which you may as well throw into the stock market if you've got such a huge appetite for risk!

• You can have more than one!

Since the cost of setting up and running an Internet Business is so low, and you can automate their operations, you can operate multiple Internet Businesses as a one-person Internet Business owner. You don't need to hire employees since your Internet Business system is doing most of the job, if not all. It works 24/7 for you. It won't call in sick. It won't give any excuses. And it definitely won't blame you if it ever had worldly problems!

• The internet is a huge market (the whole world) and it's getting bigger as you read these words

According to the Computer Industry Almanac, there were 934 million Internet users up to September 2004; there will be 1.07 billion in this year. Now, is there any doubt that a 934 million-user pool is a very attractive target given the leverage you have on the Internet?

The 4 Required Traits of an Online Business Success

Even if your business has been around for years, getting back to the basics will help you pinpoint areas you have overlooked in the past, and help you build a stronger business for the future.

The four keys to your business success are:

• Mindset

• Focus

• Education,

• Action.

Mindset

The way you think, directly affects the results you get from your business. If you look at your business as a hobby, you will make a hobby income. If you treat your business as the professional entity that it is, your income will match your expectations. Although it may seem like psycho-babble, the way you think and view your business has a huge effect on whether you can actually buy your shiny yellow Corvette, or whether you can only afford the gas.

Here's your new mindset: You are the President and CEO of your own company. It doesn't matter if you are the only person in your company, and your company consists of a 10-year-old computer sitting in the dusty corner of your bedroom. No one cares about your company except you. Your customers only care what your company can provide for them.

Next, take a realistic look at what you want to achieve. It's easy to see the success stories online and get caught up in the excitement. But look behind the scenes to see what actually happened to achieve those successes. There was a lot of groundwork that went into creating the results you read about. The money is there, but it takes some work to get to it.

To prove this point, we'll look at TheBusinessProfessional.com. One of the milestones in the company's history was generating $41,439 in sales in 17 days. But there's more to the story.

The Business Professional was born almost 2 years before the first major sales achievement. Originally, it was an online portal with a print quality magazine. Then it was transformed into a membership website.

The sales were generated, for the most part, by affiliates. The affiliates made a 50% commission, so $20,000 was paid to them. After payment processing fees, hosting and other miscellaneous fees, there was approximately $20,000 left to run the business and draw an income. So as Paul Harvey used to say, "Now you know the rest of the story."

So when you see stories of large amounts of money in short periods of time, keep in mind there is always a story behind the story. Remember to keep your expectations realistic.

Look at your business as if you were climbing a ladder. You have to lift your foot up to the first rung before you can reach the second rung. You have to make your first $10 sale before you make your first $100 sale. You have to experience your first $100 month before you have your first $500 month.

With perseverance and the right mindset, you can reach your goals, but you have to walk before you can run.

Focus

The next battle you're going to wage is with your mind. You need to stay focused on one task at a time. Pinpoint your focus to stay effective. When you sit at your computer, you are there to get a job done. There are hundreds of distractions online and offline, but you need to focus on the task at hand or your work will never get completed.

We all suffer from information overload. When you are online, it's easy to start out with great intentions of completing a task like answering email, and 2 hours later find yourself surfing mindlessly. You click on a link in an email that takes you to a website that leads you to another website with intriguing information in a link that... you get the picture. We've all been there. So you need to guard your focus and not lose sight of what you're actually supposed to be doing while you are sitting in front of your computer screen.

You have invested in this course to learn how to tap into the financial power of the internet, so focus on the course and ignore everything else for the time being. You will build a solid business faster by keeping your focus.

To prove this point, look at the results of a recent experiment. Whether you agree or disagree with the methodology, the outcome is fascinating.

Start Earning from Your Online Business

An experiment was conducted with a group of mentally challenged people. Each person had the ability to listen to simple instructions and carry out a simple task. None of them could do more than one simple task at a time, but all of them were able to complete menial tasks on a computer.

The top person in the group had been taught how to copy and paste text from a Word document into a simple form on a website. Each day, he would sit down at the computer for 20 minutes, copy and paste exactly as he'd been shown and then turn off the computer. This was his "job" every single day, day-in, day-out. The text he was copying and pasting from the Word document into the form on the website was a simple article. He was given a new article each morning to copy into an article submission website and then push the send button. That was all he did. That was all he knew how to do. He didn't suffer from information overload. He simply followed the instructions he had been given. Each article promoted a website. After 3 weeks of sending out one article a day, the website made its' first sale, then another and another until the website was making at least one sale a day.

If a mentally challenged person can generate sales from a website, using one simple tactic, so can you. The key to making it happen is focus – your focus.

Narrow your focus and block out all the other noise in your life. Focus on this course until it is crystal clear and follow each step exactly as it's presented. Do not hop around, don't get side tracked, don't get bogged down with information. Follow the steps in the order they have been presented and you will have a solid business that you are proud of.

Education

Now that you have the proper mindset and you are focused, let's move into training mode. This is the third key to unlocking your business success. The course you are taking right now is your education. By the time you are finished this course, you'll know exactly how to set up, run and profit from your online business.

As you take your business to new levels of profitability, you want to keep learning and advancing. It's beneficial to read a business publication or listen to a business audio for at least half an hour each day. This way, you are continuing your education daily, but also working on your business. Educate yourself every day, but make sure you put your education into action. Don't get stuck in education mode and forget to act on your new knowledge.

Action

This is the vital key to success. You need to pare down your actions. Your only productive business actions are the ones that are helping to increase your business. The rest is wasting valuable action time. Surfing the internet is not a productive action unless you are researching new opportunities. If you are researching, you need to limit your surfing to include only the subject matter that is essential to making decisions. It's very easy to get sidetracked and waste hours upon hours and getting nothing productive accomplished. You need to concentrate and stay focused.

If you have a home-based business, you need to effectively set some time every day as your business time. No one should disturb you during that time. You have to discipline yourself to keep that time as business time.

Start Earning from Your Online Business

Before you sit down at your computer, decide what you want to accomplish. If you want to write an autoresponder message and update your website with a new article, those are your priorities. Talking to your friends on Skype, and surfing for irrelevant information can be done after you have accomplished your goals.

If you are able to sit down at your computer undisturbed for several hours, break your time into blocks to ensure you maximize your effectiveness. The most important part of your business is your marketing. It should be the very first thing you do.

If you have 3 hours, your schedule could look like this:

Hour 1: Write and submit an article (marketing)

Hour 2: Edit a report (project development)

Hour 3: Answer email (administration)

Your daily actions will determine how successful your business is and how quickly you join the ranks of the high-level income earners. If you don't set up little mini plans for yourself, each time you sit down at the computer, you will easily waste your time and accomplish little or nothing.

Don't confuse activity with accomplishment.

CHAPTER 2- PLAN AND DOCUMENT YOUR BUSINESS IDEAS

Your online business plan needs to make sure it addresses the management and administration structure – in other words your organization's breakdown. Online businesses often have a simpler organization structure than a traditional business, but that's not always the case, and it must be clearly defined.

You will need to cover the management structure and ownership of your business. It's okay if one person fills a number of roles. Online businesses that are starting up often don't have more than one or two people running the whole business.

During the startup period, the owner is not going to be receiving a paycheck or any benefits. Initially owner salaries are going to be figured out based on the profitability of the company but they should never be more than fifty percent of the profit of the business.

If the company is limited, there will be the distribution of shares among the owners. That could be one person, two people or more, but the breakdown needs to be included in the business plan so potential investors know and understand the business structure.

You will also need to include the managerial style that you plan to use. This should be broken out so that not just investors but business owners can stay on track and later compare.

- Communication - Communication will be mainly through, i.e. email, texting, oral, etc.

- Decisions Making - Who is going to be the final decision maker for all the decisions pertaining to your business?

- Project Management –There are different styles. You should define what style you are going to use. For example, all project management will be defined by the PMI PMBOK standards.

- Record Keeping – The company will use <insert accounting package name> to manage our financial records.

You will need to define the management structure. For example, Person A will be President, Director of Marketing, and Director of IT. Person B will be Director of Operations, Director of Finance. You are then going to define what the responsibilities are in each of those positions that a person holds. Be clear and concise when describing these roles, because you will be using this yourself in running your business.

The organization breakdown is going to look very different from one business to the next, so make sure that you take the time to properly define what your business organization is going to look like.

Market + Metrics = Your Online Business Plan

You are going to want to specifically focus on the users and your demographics that you plan to hit with your new online business and how your costs and price compare to what the market is currently willing to pay for the product or service you are going to offer.

It's here that you are going to take the time to make a list of your current competition along with what you feel they are doing correctly and what they are doing wrong. This is one of the most important sections for luring lenders and investors on-board with your plan. If you aren't able to show that you have an idea that's innovative and that you also have the marketing strategy to shoot you forward, you'll have difficulty getting any investment interest.

In the business landscape today, your ideas need to also make sure to include social media strategies such as Twitter, Facebook, LinkedIn, etc. Your business personality needs to shine through here and if you know the magic to help this happen in social media, you are definitely on the right path. When you are able to locate influencers that's how you will discover those people who are linked to what you have to offer or who can help you to identify the impact you will have on society.

Online entrepreneurs are lucky to be able to make use of metrics. This is something that businesses in the past did not have access to. This instantly lets you measure how your business is doing. It shows how successful you are in a very inexpensive and practical manner. These are very easy to obtain.

Sure, it's nice to read what your online customers are saying; however, this does not tell you whether a person is actually buying the product you have to offer. The easiest and most effective way to measure success is by paying attention to how your business is performing with those individuals that you have already established a relationship with. This will give you some good feedback about just how effective your online business actually is.

It's important that your business plan pays adequate attention to those marketing factors in combination with the use of metrics to ensure that your marketing is actually working the way you believed it would. Remember once you look at your metrics, this is a good time to 'fine tune' any necessary changes that you think you need to make.

Management + Financial Summary = Online Business Plan

You are creating your business plan for your online business and like all business plans there are a number of sections you need to put together to ensure you have a plan you can follow to keep your business on track and headed for successes. You may be surprised to learn that many business plans come up short in their management and financial summary. Perhaps this is simply because they are unsure.

Start by creating an outline of what type of experience you want to see your management team have. How many people you envision on your management team, the individual roles that they will have and what their responsibilities will be individually and as a team.

Think of the management summary as hiring resume where you can easily see the qualifications you are looking for, the work history of those that will be involved in the startup of your business. If it's a smaller venture like so many online businesses are, you may have to wear many different hats yourself and improve your skills in some areas. You may not have the luxury of having many people on your management team and so in these instances, in addition to you having to have a wide range of skills, the people you do hire may have to be able to perform a broader range of tasks.

In addition to taking the time to outline what your management team will look like you need to also address any financing that you have put into place and that's ready to go for your startup. Your working capital is critical to your startup. How much working capital you need will depend on your specific venture. Some companies have little to no stock on hand while others carry huge amounts.

Sales and revenues are established by you for the business plan; however, we all that these projections can be way off if the person creating the business plan isn't being realistic, so try to keep it real. Your business plan is also going to establish how much capital you already have and what your operating costs will be.

What's nice about an online business, is that if you don't any sales yet so you can't provide solid sales numbers, you can get your website up and running, go live, get things moving on the site in a practical way that's closer to reality and then show the potential investors what you are making and what you're spending.

Bottom line – make sure your business plan thoroughly details your management and financial needs.

What is The Right Business for Your Skills?

Don't even consider creating your formal business plan until you are actually ready to use it. The business plan of today for online businesses is far less formal than it used to be and it is far more practical. Does each section of your business plan when you require it and don't be too concerned about formalities?

Don't confuse this with scrapping out your business plan completely, because online entrepreneurs still need to focus on whatever their 'niche' is and their plans for getting their business both off the ground and growing.

What's in your business plan can change based on the current situation, what you will incorporate into your business plan won't change. So in other words your final destination will remain the same but how you reach that destination can change.

How to Create an Online Business Plan

The internet is an extremely powerful tool for all kinds of companies and it has certainly changed the kinds of companies that will prosper. There are four key reasons for an internet site:

1. Transactional

2. Content

3. Promotional

4. Relational

These apply no matter what kind of business you are operating. Remember that your business plan is alive – that blueprint is a living, breathing entity that can help you to navigate. It can help you to manage your business, help you find potential partners or investors, help you find lenders and others who can see your business plan and easily understand it.

Your business plan will need to include an executive summary, company overview, business offering, marketing plan and marketing analysis, strategy and implementation of that strategy, what your management team will look like, and finally your financial projections.

It's important that you understand your online market and that you are able to clearly and concisely create a picture of what this will look like for those who will be reading your business plan and making decisions based on it, and who may not have a good understanding of online business opportunities.

Just because you are running, an online business or planning to start an online business does not mean that you do not need a business plan. Every viable business should have a business plan, even if they are not interested in gaining investment capital. This finely detailed plan will help you to navigate through the waters, and help you to not only get your business off the ground but also keep it successfully moving forward.

Use a One-Page Sales Pitch to Introduce Your Business

You are about to start an online business and you know it's a great idea that promises great success. You've done your homework, you've crunched the numbers and you are ready to create your business plan. Now all you need is an investor, venture capitalist or lender to step up. But how are you going to make your business proposal stand out against the many others. How are you going to make your business plan get noticed?

You want to create a professional pitch page your business on a single page. Now we've called it a sales pitch and while technically it's not a 'sales pitch' in a roundabout way it is – you want to sell investors on what you have to offer so that they are interested enough to read your entire business plan.

Your single page sales pitch can come in the form of your executive summary. Your executive summary is the last thing you write and the first thing they read. If you can't capture their interest here, you will have lost your bid to capture their interest. So make sure you are getting potential investors and others who will read your business plan excited about your business, but remember you have to make sure you aren't exaggerating or fluffing up the facts.

Instead focus on the most important facts that are in your business plan, present them in an appealing way, and point out whenever you have the opportunity why what you have is exciting and should tantalize investors. You can also create what's called a professional pitch page.

Let's have a look at what that page can include. This professional pitch page can be shared with investors, lenders, advisers and business partners.

Your pitch will let you highlight the following:

• Your company summary

• Any market problems

• Solutions

• Your established sales channels

Karen Turner

• Marketing activities

• Your target market

• Your market size

• Your competition

• What is your competitive advantage?

• Your funding requirements

• The big picture for your financial projections

• Your main milestones

• Your team members

If you had just 60 seconds to sell your business to investors, how would you do it? What would it look like? What would you say? When you are creating your professional pitch page keep this in mind. It will help you to focus and provide the most relevant information.

CHAPTER 3- USING EXISTING INTERNET BUSINESS MODELS FOR YOUR BUSINESS VENTURE

The 19 Killer Internet Businesses listed below form the basic foundation upon which most Internet Riches are made by the one-person Entrepreneur. Some of them involve more TIME than money to run. Some of them involve more money than time. Some of them require you to have a very good writing ability that you may have. Some of them don't require you to write well or at all. Some of them have many ways of making money, which may be what you're very keen on. Some of them only have one or two ways of making money, which you may prefer to avoid. Some of them require you to sell something while others don't require you to sell anything and still make you money. Some of them don't require you to even have a web site. Others don't even require that you have your own computer, which may be an even better thing for you.

Karen Turner

If you don't find the "Freebie" Internet Business Model is for you, you have another 18 more to choose. Not every Internet Business Model will suit everyone but the whole gamut of Internet Business Models has been presented. With different, killer 19 Internet Business Models to choose from, there are Internet Business Models to suit every temperament.

Quite simply – there is a different Internet Business for everybody.

So what are the Internet Businesses?

INTERNET BUSINESS MODEL No. 1

This business model is known better as the "Retailer" model. How would you like to own your own Internet Store selling over 1 million products if you wish, with nothing to stock or fulfill? Just imagine - no real store overheads, no need to employ hundreds of staff, and no real-estate rental charges! This Internet Business Model also has two very attractive Profit Centers that are not directly related to the products themselves.

INTERNET BUSINESS MODEL No. 2

Aptly called the "Killer Sales Letter" Model, here you can make money with just a single webpage! This Internet Business Model is favored by a lot of Savvy Internet Entrepreneurs out there. At first glance, all you see is just a single web page. But there's more to it than meets the eye. Some swear by this model, others find it too much of a bother. Find out what both groups see.

INTERNET BUSINESS MODEL No. 3

Send out e-mail regularly without spamming to people willing to pay you for it! This is one of the lowest costs Internet Business Model you can do. It's especially suitable for certain individuals.

INTERNET BUSINESS MODEL No. 4

Give out 20 characters of letters of the alphabet to people willing to pay you for it. Some of them actually create this model on the fly while being funded by the money that is coming in from their initial sales of those characters!

INTERNET BUSINESS MODEL No. 5

This is known as the "virus" model. ICQ is an example of this Internet Business Model. This Internet Business Model can be explosive if done right. All you need to have is a single page web site that features something funny, sad touching, rude or controversial. Then your visitors who see your website will not be able to resist telling their friends about it. When their friends see it too, they will in turn tell their friends about it, and on and on it goes. There are those who have this Model on their site but do not realize it at all! Your profits come from many sources. This can be one of the easiest Models to set up, depending on your aspirations and content.

INTERNET BUSINESS MODEL No. 6

Gather people from all over the world together to talk to each other for free and make money in the process! This can be one of the most enjoyable Internet Business Models to do. You are also able to leverage your efforts through the efforts of some members of your group for free.

INTERNET BUSINESS MODEL No. 7

Be the only site to go to on your area of interest, and earn prestige as well as money in the process! This Internet Business Model fits certain individuals like a glove - they wouldn't want to trade it for anything else!

INTERNET BUSINESS MODEL No. 8

Provide the right tools for your visitors to use and make money in the process! Give your visitors a very useful tool to use and they'll make money for you in more ways than one. Your tool can sometimes be found readily available all over the Internet!

INTERNET BUSINESS MODEL No. 9

This is the "Freebie" Internet Business Model we've covered briefly in this special report. Provide free stuff to people all begging you to do it every day to make money. One Super Internet Entrepreneur makes hundreds of thousands of dollars every year by just sending jokes 5 days a week to his subscribers.

INTERNET BUSINESS MODEL No. 10

If you're an expert, trainer, guru, consultant or speaker of some kind, this is the perfect model for you. There are 8 different ways of making money with this Internet Business Model, one of which is so little-known but so full of money-making potential that you'll be kicking yourself if you don't implement it!

INTERNET BUSINESS MODEL No. 11

You don't have to be a professional or degree holder to be a consultant to others under this Internet Business Model. All it requires is some time and effort and the right strategies and tactics.

INTERNET BUSINESS MODEL No. 12

Prepare yourself to trash your competition all selling products similar to yours! This is the "Super Affiliate" Internet Business Model. You can easily outshine, out-click and outgun your competitors using specific, little-used techniques and be the shining star even if everybody else sells the same thing as you are – if you know EXACTLY what to do.

INTERNET BUSINESS MODEL No. 13

Make your worn pair of Levi's and Nike's make a fortune for you using the Internet. The Super Internet Entrepreneurs under this category are called "Power Sellers". They use a little ingenuity and plenty of tools found on the Internet to help them make their fortune.

INTERNET BUSINESS MODEL No. 14

Become a millionaire by just playing with the letters of the alphabet. You don't even need to create a web site for this one. A good example is Business.com. Business.com sold for over USD7 million some years ago. Those days are long gone, but if you what to do, you can purchase domain names for less than USD10 and resell them for at least 10 or 100 times more, and having willing buyers waiting to buy them from you.

INTERNET BUSINESS MODEL No. 15

If you're into Multi-Level-Marketing (also known as MLM or Network Marketing), there is no bigger or better medium for you to use than the Internet to help you recruit and sell your products. The total Internet population as of September 2004 was about 934 million. The figure is projected to reach 1.07 billion in Year 2005. With the Internet being global in nature, your downlines can from all over the world! I know of an Internet Entrepreneur who had 215 paid downlines within 4 weeks after joining an Internet MLM, and 4 weeks after that he had 305 paid members! How long does it take you to recruit 305 paid downlines in conventional MLM?

INTERNET BUSINESS MODEL No. 16

This is the Reseller Rights Business we have covered in this report. Put a super twist to an existing way of making money on the Internet to come up with an equally explosive new Internet Business Model. This relatively new Internet Business Model being used only by a handful of Super Internet Entrepreneurs so far. It requires some work but well worth it for one particular profit center it can create for you.

INTERNET BUSINESS MODEL No. 17

If you're a technical person or a programmer, this Model is for you. You make money by giving your software away to webmasters for free!

INTERNET BUSINESS MODEL No. 18

This model enables you to fully automate a service you would normally provide to your customers in the real world. When you can automate a service, you're no longer bound by the number of hours you have in a day. With the Internet, you can deliver your service to an entire world in the same time!

INTERNET BUSINESS MODEL No. 19

You make money by simply thanking your visitors for having done something on the Internet! Quite simply, you target webmasters with a free online tool that will end up with the webmasters visitors looking at your "Thank You for Using This Tool" page. The "Thank You" page is where you make your money!

While there are several different Internet Business Models, it also means that their marketing strategies are different all together. For example, assume you're a plumber in the physical world. So how would you promote your services? You would place ads in the newspapers and in the Yellow Pages. But if you're running a hot dog cart, you don't have to advertise your hot dog cart in the papers. You just need to locate your hot dog cart in high-trafficked areas such as the shopping complex, outside a movie theatre and so forth.

The conclusion is this: different Internet Business Models are for different people. If you're to start your own Internet Business, be sure to choose one that suits you best! There you go! Now, you might want to ask me "what does a successful business actually look like?" That is a good and very important question. Because a good way to learn and become successful yourself is to imitate what other successful people are doing.

Chapter 4- Info Products That Sell Online

The information explosion that has taken over the world through the availability of the Internet is truly a mixed blessing – it comes with the following benefits and drawbacks:

• People have ready access to information but do not have enough time to read it.

• There are so many types of information competing of attention.

• There is an increasing number of competition selling low-cost information products.

So while the rewards may be great and lucrative for some, the competition is stiffer than ever before. The best way to tackle this challenge is to do your homework and learn about the industry as much as you can. This will help you decide which particular niche to target, how to best position your products and what the most effective way to present it is.

Types of Information Products

But first things first – what are the options available to you when it comes to selling information products? Below are the most popular and highly in demand information products in the market today:

•Ebooks

Ebooks or electronic/digital books are easily the most common and in demand type of information products available today. This is probably because it is the easiest and cheapest for of information product to can sell and buy. There are so many eBooks available on the market today, covering every imaginable topic and catering to different audience.

If you have a flair for writing or you feel you can be able to share expert advice and information on a specific field, you can consider creating your own eBook and sell it in the market. But of course, not any eBook will do. You will want to come up with one that will best appeal to your target audience. Here are the popular ones for your reference:

How-To Tips and Information

This type of eBook offers important assistance on learning a new skill, enhance existing knowledge or provide an innovative approach to doing certain things. It can cover different topics such as cars, bookkeeping, playing the piano, cooking, learning a new language, attracting women and so much more.

If you plan on creating a how-to eBook, you should first take time to study your target audience and find out what are the most significant concerns/issues/problems and create content that will be able to provide a solution to that problem. In order to do that, you will need to conduct extensive study on your market and determine how you can effectively position your information product to be regarded as the ultimate solution to the problem.

Making Money Info

Another type of eBook is one that is geared towards offering information on how to make money. This eBook for one is an example of that kind of information product. Most people, if not all are always interested in new ways of generating new income streams, especially in view of the difficult and unstable economy. If you have discovered how to make it big and rake in serious amount of money doing something, then you might want to write about it and share your expertise.

Money Saving Info

Aside from making money, people are generally interested on how to save money. Well, it actually makes total sense, right? No matter how much money you make, you will eventually exhaust your resources, sooner or later. With so many people facing debt problems, debt issues, every penny counts – which means, an eBook on saving one, whether it is on learning how to get better gas mileage or maximizing grocery coupons, can prove to be highly interesting. Health and Fitness

With the growing prevalence of fatal and life-altering diseases, a lot of people have grown more concerned about their health and general well-being. This type of eBook covers various topics such as weight loss, natural remedies and muscle gain. Through the years, there will always be a great market for these information products.

These type of eBooks focus on providing relationship advice, such as dealing with a divorce or getting back an ex. There have been growing demands for books that tackle gaining self-confidence, dealing with stress, and becoming a better person.

Training and Skills Improvement

Whether people are genuinely interested in acquiring a new skill or trying to save money by doing things on their own, more and more people seek online resources on enhancing knowledge and improving a certain skill. This may include Photoshop tutorials or the basics of knitting.

Travel and Lifestyle Guides

There will always be a constant demand for books that provide information on a certain area, city or country. If you are confident you will be able to provide valuable information on a certain place, why not create an eBook to provide information and insider knowledge about the place focusing on specific topics, tourists and visitors are most likely interested to know.

• **Video Tutorials**

Another type of information product that you can sell is video tutorials, which of course, provides information, depending on the particular topic you want to pursue. If you plan on offering training courses, video formats are highly recommended so you can demonstrate/discuss every step for your audience to see and observe. If your demonstration involves navigating around the web or certain software, a screen casting software can be used to record every cursor action. A lot of people prefer video tutorials over written ones as it is easier to understand and it comes with better visual appeal, which is ideal for people who prefer watching instead of reading. Of course, there is also the fact that people can play and replay video tutorials whenever they need to.

• Online Courses

This is a high end information product that is essentially a course or a training program segmented into modules. In order to create one, you will need to come up with a general theme that can help solve a specific problem or teach clients about something that they are genuinely interested of knowing.

The structure of online courses can greatly vary, depending on the topic and scope. These are typically offered live or can be delivered via email. It is recommended to stick to 8 lessons/modules or possibly lesser than that since according to studies the average attention space will start to wane after 6 to 8 lessons.

• Membership Sites

As the name suggests, you can basically make money by setting up a membership site and attract users to sign up. Membership sites are not to be considered a passive income stream as it can require constant work and interaction. This is perhaps a viable venue to make money as it is one of the most overlooked income opportunity and a well-known lucrative business model.

• Software Development

Among the different forms of information products, software development is the most expensive one that will require a significant investment. However, if you have a certain idea or concept that is designed to respond to a need or provide a solution to a problem, you can potentially hit a goldmine. Truth is there is so much money that can be made in software development. Some people would say, "I'm not technical" or I don't know a thing about programming" but the thing is, the highly successful people who raked in millions of dollars off software products are not programmers but businessmen, with brilliant ideas who relentlessly pursued great, innovative ideas.

So these are the top money making channels for selling information products. At this point, you may think to yourself, "I don't think I can pursue any of these" and come up with a number of reasons such as "I don't know how to write or code" or " I don't have any brilliant ideas to sell", well, think again.

Money does not grow on trees and nothing comes for free these days. If you are keen on gaining that financial freedom – whether you're preparing for retirement or looking for a means to get out of the corporate rat race -- read the remaining chapters. Discover how you can sell information products through strategic planning and innovative thinking.

What Topics to Write?

So how do you decide what topics best appeal to your target market and which one will you be most effective in? Here are some factors to take into account:

Something You Are Expert In or Passionate About

Aside from the motivation of generating income, you should also take into consideration your personal passions in order to come up with an information product that sells. It must be something that you believe in, which you are eager to share or confident to sell an idea which you believe will present real value or solution to your target audience.

If making money is your motivating factor, you may run the risk of selling information that does not offer real value at the expense of your buyers. Take time to identify what your interests are, what topics do you consider yourself an expert in or something that you can truly identify with?

Research Topics That Are Popular In the Market

If you have already identified what topic you want to focus on, you will need to drive down and identify a specific issue/problem that most people in your target market can identify with. So aside from taking into account your personal passions, you should also take time to study what best appeals to your target audience – the same ones you will be selling your information product to. This will help you ensure that the information product you want to create actually has a defined market for it and not merely take on a hit and miss approach.

For example, if you are a mother yourself and you are truly passionate about parenting and helping working mothers juggle work and family life as well as setting aside time to nurture oneself, study on that particular market. What are the common, prevailing woes?

What issues do they usually deal with? You may want to focus on instilling discipline among toddlers in this modern world or maybe a potty training guide.

Spend Time in Forums and Social Media Sites

In order to best appeal to your target audience, you need to get intimate – take time to study who these people are, what are their common problems, what do they usually spend on, what is their average monthly income, how do they spend their leisure time, etc.

So how do you exactly achieve this important information without conducting an extensive survey? Make good use of social media sites and forums. Facebook and Twitter have search functions that you can use to filter search results. You can also determine what specific age bracket you want to target.

By hearing the questions and learning what they are talking about straight from your target audience, you will be able to come up with an effective content strategy that can best appeal to that specific niche.

Twitter Search Function

With almost everyone on Twitter these days, it's the perfect place to study your target market. Using the search function, key in the topic you want to work on and include a question mark sign in your search. For example "yoga", this will generate a result tweets with questions users posted about yoga. This will help you have a 'pulse' on the current interests/concerns.

Facebook

Since most Facebook users use privacy restrictions, you can conduct a study on the Fan pages of your competitors or top industry providers of products or services that are relevant to the information product you plan on working on. Try to come up with

Karen Turner

top 3 competitor fan pages that have the most number of "likes" and take time to read interactions.

Forums

Forums offer a wealth of information. Find one that is specifically created for the market you want to target. For example, you can find forums on working mothers through a simple Google search. Spend time reading what the members are talking about, what concerns and problems aired and advices sought.

Information products go beyond delivering relevant information. To be really effective, you need to deliver real value. By taking time to study your market and what are the common concerns, you will be able to outline your content that will best address the problems and appeal to your target audience.

CHAPTER 5- STEPS TO BUILDING AN ONLINE BUSINESS –FAST!

To set specific goals for your new business, first ask yourself this question: Why do I want to start an Internet Business? We already covered this in the early chapter, which is why you're reading on! Okay, next question: What product or service can I offer to the people on the Internet? **OR** Do I have a product or service that people are looking for on the Internet? To save you some research work, I've included the list of Top 17 Best-selling items / categories on the Internet below:

1. Clothing

2. Toys and Video Games

3. Electronics

4. Computer Hardware

5. VCDs / DVDs

6. Books

7. Greeting Cards

8. Home Furnishing

9. Jewelry

10. Health

11. Travel

12. Automobile

13. Real Estate

14. Online Trading

15. Music

16. Food

17. Sports

When identifying a need, doing market research is part of your homework. One of your first steps should be to find out what it means to do business online and to determine the best ways for you to fit into the exploding field of e-commerce (electronic commerce). The more information you have on the following aspects of the Internet, the more likely you are to succeed in doing business online:

Competition:

Familiarize yourself with other existing Internet Businesses that are already doing what you want to do.

Customers:

Research the various kinds of customers who shop online and who might visit your site.

Environment:

Explore the special language and style of online communication – in other words, know the culture of the Internet. If you are not yet familiar with the culture of the Internet, then the best way to learn is to subscribe to e-zines (electronic magazines) and newsletters for your reading. Write all your ideas down on a piece of paper. Ask yourself, "What do I have that people are looking for on the Internet?" Take your time. This is not supposed to be an overnight activity. So, don't be surprised if you take days. Taking your time and doing a thorough market research on the Internet beats jumping onto an opportunity at first sight.

Picking an online business model

Already decided what you have in store for your customers? Good! The next thing to do on the list is to choose the right Internet Business Model. Now this is crucial to your Internet Business success.

The Internet Business Model has to be right for the type of product or service you're offering to your customers. When choosing the right Internet Business Model, you will want to take the following factors into consideration:

Karen Turner

• Profit Margin – the higher the profit margin, the better.

• Delivery – can be easily delivered to your customers via a system.

• Shipping Cost – as low as possible or even none.

• Marketing – different Internet Business Models have different marketing strategies. Choose the model that has the best marketing strategy for your product or services.

To date, there are 19 low-cost, high-profit Internet Business Models on the Internet to choose from.

Identify your target market

The inside secret is to search in search engines (such as Google and Overture) with keywords related to your product or service to find out if many websites, newsletters and community groups focus on this interest.

Get a domain name

I have already explained to you what a domain name is. You also know that your website address can ALSO be your Internet Business name.

You will want to take out another new piece of paper again to write down ALL the keywords related to your Internet Business. You see, you want your domain name to:

• be short and easy to remember (and catchy, too!),

• be relevant to the product or service you're selling,

- include keywords of your product or service to improve search engine rankings.

For example, if you want to sell a product teaching people how to break-dance, then you will want to start writing down all the keywords related to break-dance. For starters, write 100 keywords. What next, you ask? Write some more! Write 200 or 300 if you have to. The more keywords, the better. That is because this is a one-off activity. And remember that you will be using this domain name for a very long time, if not forever.

Now, don't even get lazy. Okay, I'll offer you some food for thought. Are you parent to any child? If you are not, then imagine you are one right now. You and your spouse have a child for the first time. You and your spouse would want to give the best name to your child, right? Of course you both would! You and your spouse would brainstorm on giving your child the best name. "How about John?" "Aw, John is too common a name!" "Then how about ...?" "I think the name..." and finally, your child has a name to be addressed by.

When brainstorming on your child's name, you and your spouse consciously or unconsciously know that giving your child the best and meaningful name is VERY important because your child will be living with that name from cradle to the grave. So, on the same token, why would you not think the same when brainstorming on a good domain name? This is your Internet Business. You need to nurture and grow it during its infancy stages before it rewards you. Are you not going to give it your best attention, too? I hope that woke you up.

Now, back to the keyword activity... With the help of the list of keywords you have written down, you will find it easy to get a domain name that fulfills the 3 guidelines stated above.

Next, check whether the domain name has been registered or not. If the domain name has been registered by someone else, you will have to use another domain name. So, maybe you'll think of using www.lordofthefloor.com for a domain name. When brainstorming on a good domain name, be sure to come up with at least a few names in case the domain name you wish to use is already taken.

Remember me telling you that there can never be two houses bearing the same address? Another thing you have to consider is the various kinds of domain names on the Internet. So you will have to choose carefully. Below are some of the common ones:

- **.com-** stands for commercial / community. The most overused domain entity on the Internet. This is recommended for your Internet Business.

- **.net-** stands for network.

- **.org-** stands for organization. A lot of online communities use this domain entity.

- **.gov-** stands for government. All government web sites use this domain entity.

- **.biz-** stands for business. This is recommended for your Internet Business.

The next thing to do is find a web host. Any business needs a place to call home. If you run a conventional business, you have to rent space in an office or shopping complex. In the case of setting up an Internet Business, you need to set up a virtual space. You do so by creating a website and finding a host for your site.

Start Earning from Your Online Business

A web host company that makes your site available 24/7 (24 hours a day, 7 days a week) by maintaining it on a Web server. I have covered this topic with you briefly in the second chapter. When sourcing for a good web host, you want to make sure that your host has a fast connection to the Internet and can handle large numbers of simultaneous visits (also known as hits) that your website is sure to get eventually.

You also want to make sure that your web host offers a variety of related services, including some or all of the following:

- E-mail addresses. You're like to be able to get several e-mail addresses for your own. Many web hosts also give you special e-mail addresses called autoresponders (discussed earlier in Chapter 2).

- Domain name. You and I have just covered this subject above.

- Web page software. Some web hosting services include web page authoring / editing software.

- Multimedia / CGI scripts. Some web hosting services have the ability to serve complex and memory-intensive content such as RealAudio sound files or RealVideo video clips. They also let you process web page forms that you include on your site by executing computer programs called CGI scripts.

- Shopping Cart software. Most organizations prove you with Web page forms that you can fill out to create sale items and offer them in an online shopping cart.

- Site statistics. Site statistics give you an idea of how many visitors you have received.

• Shopping and electronic commerce features and more.

Make a simple and professional website

Since you're into business, the purpose of your website is to SELL. Nothing else! That's because YOUR WEBSITE SHOULD HAVE ONE MAIN FOCUS. Nope, it's not selling dozens or hundreds of products. Nope, it's not links to several different affiliate programs and NOPE, certainly not a link to Yahoo.com. Doing any of the above just confuses your visitor, thus decreasing your chances of converting him or her into your customer. If you're selling a product or service, it should be clear what ONE action you want them to take. They would either:

• **Buy your product or service**

OR

• **Don't buy**

But are you going to let them go away just like that? Of course **N-E-V-E-R!** So, you need to get your visitors to leave their e-mail address and other essential information for follow-up increases your chance to help you make a sale because the fact is that most people don't buy on first contact. To do this, you write a compelling sales letter for your product and post it to your website. You can add images of your product, testimonials from happy customers, and other relevant images. The focus of your website is the sales letter.

Now, let's talk about the layout of your web page. Your main text color should be black on a white background. You can have other colors such as blue, red and gray on your website, but the background behind the text should be white. The color of your main text should be black. No other exceptions! That is because this is the easiest format to read. You are in business so dress your site in a business manner.

On the technical side, you can choose from three methods to create your own web pages:

• **Do it yourself (D.I.Y.)** – if you are well versed in using web page tools such as Macromedia Dreamweaver and Microsoft FrontPage to create your web pages then this option is probably the best for you.

• **Hire A Free Lancer, Professional or Internal I.T. Team** - if you don't know how to create web pages, you may want to consider hiring professional help as learning how to create your own web pages can be time-consuming. While it can incur high professional fee, this option can be your best value for money in the long run. However, this option should be filtered out if you're on a strict budget.

• **Go to Solobis** – if the above two methods are not for you – don't sweat over it. This suite has been set up to remove not only the technical barriers but also eliminate risks for aspiring but clueless Internet Entrepreneurs at an affordable price. Besides having over 400 beautiful web site templates to choose from, this suite provides other Internet Business tools and services such as Sequential Autoresponders, Pop-Up Window Generator, Mailing List Broadcaster, Article Generator, Killer Sales Letter Generator, Headline Generator, and many more to get you starting your Internet Business quickly! If you are on a strict budget, then all the more you must go to this suite to make your dreams of earning income from the Internet come to life!

Karen Turner

Create a unique selling proposition (USP) for you product / website.

Find ways to make your business stand out from the crowd. Make yourself and your web site unique in some way and providing things that others don't offer. They can be as tangible as half-price sales, contests, seasonal sales, freebies or reports. They can also make your business site higher in quality than the rest. That is important because there really is no purpose of your Internet Business to exist if you have a million visitors coming to view your site but too few of them actually become your customers (a conversion rate of less than 1% is rated poor). Here's what you can do to create your own USP. Take a brand new piece of paper and write, "I know how most..." Then, half-way down the page, write "Well, what I do is..."

The purpose of this activity is to know how most businesses in your field are in the first place and then you write what tells you and your Internet Business apart from them. This will take a while to do. Checking on your competition's USP is part of the activity, too.

Next, you will want to write out many phrases or sentences. This can take days but it will be worth it for your Internet Business in the long run. Once you have just the right phrase, which will be your USP which you will use to separate you from all of the competition. Now, that is what I call UNIQUE!

Write sales copy that gets results!

Your website must be treated as a sales letter, not a brochure. That's because brochures don't sell. Let me repeat – BROCHURES DON'T SELL. Brochures just inform theirs viewers of a product or service. But they won't help you make even a sale (unless that is really what you want but hey, I have yet to meet anyone who wants to be in business to lose sales!). Your sales letter consists of primarily:

• **Headline**

• **Sub-headline**

• **Benefits vs. Features**

• **USP**

• **Free / Special Offer**

You have to find a headline that will grab the attention of your visitors or else they will not read the rest of your sales letter. This is very crucial – the headline will make or break your sales letter! Assuming, you're selling an instructional video on how to play soccer professionally, so you must come up with an attention-grabbing headline for your product like the following: *"Learn To Play Soccer Like A Pro In Just 7 Days"* Visitors especially Soccer enthusiasts (but not pros) would definitely stop dead in their tracks and read on to learn more about your product. Notice the upper-cased and highlighted words.

WARNING: Do not give false promises or mention something you cannot or don't intend to deliver in your sales letter in the attempt to get your customers to buy from you. This is important business practice regardless of any form of business you are doing. For instance, if this product cannot guarantee its students to be a Soccer professional in a week, then the product should be named otherwise or not make into the lights of the day.

The **sub-headline** will encourage your visitors to read further. The sub-headline will give a spark of hope to Soccer player wannabes who couldn't help but think that their handicap is stopping them from performing like an Ace on the Soccer field and therefore encourages them to read further. Since you've already got them interested in reading your letter, the rest of your sales letter must tell your potential buyers about the benefits and features of your product. For instance, you can say that your product is the best out there (assuming that is true). You can back this fact by throwing in testimonials from happy buyers who benefited from your product, and testimonials are indeed powerful.

If you have a free offer that can help you increase the chance of making a sale, don't hesitate to give! In this case, you can give a free one-minute preview clip of your instructional video for your visitors to watch. Should your visitors decide that this is for them, they would buy from you. Now, isn't that awesome?

The 3 Types of Online Businesses to Choose From

The following are the more common types of online businesses that people are running. Keep in mind, the decision is up to you as to what type of business you want to run.

Marketing Business

This is one of the most common types of online businesses. You can either run this business by exclusively marketing your own products, or by marketing those from other companies. In order for this business to be successful, it needs to be promoted effectively to potential customers via search engines, email or other sources. We will look at marketing in more depth later in this book.

Start Earning from Your Online Business
Turnkey Internet Business

This is a very trendy type of business. You purchase a website and then run the business on a web platform that is provided by the business. In order to promote such an online business, there are many different methods you could use, such as promoting individual products or services to your online customers.

Internet Services

This is a business where specific services are provided to online customers. Many times, these businesses are set up according to a person's professional expertise. The types of businesses under this umbrella are online consulting, computer software assistance, hardware trouble shooting and even how to start an online business.

In addition to the ones mentioned above, there are many other kinds of online businesses too. You've got entertainment websites, interior design, dating, article writing, fitness, medical, online chat and the list is endless. It doesn't really matter what kind of online business ("niche") you decide to get involved in, it is important to plan carefully and have the ability promote the business professionally over the internet. The only limit is your imagination.

Chapter 6- On Marketing and Collecting Payments

Now is the time to market to your target market.

Each Internet Business Model is different. Therefore, you don't market each and every one of them the same way. The truth is, not all Internet Business Models depend on a good search engine listing. In fact, some of them are not designed to be listed by search engines at all! That is simply because each Internet Business Models have different objectives and set up. That also means they require different marketing strategies and tactics to make it work. Not knowing the different Internet Marketing approaches that are available for different Internet Business Models can be expensive. It will result in spending more time, money and effort than is necessary for promoting your Internet Business.

Tracking Sales and Site Traffic

The purpose of the last step is to determine your conversion rate of visitors into customers. This can be easily done if your web host provides a site statistic. A good conversion rate from a Killer Sales Letter is 1 – 3% (depending on the price of the product). In other words, for every 100 targeted prospects who visit your site, at least one of them will buy your product or pay access to your service. If the conversion rate is higher than 2%, then you are doing very, very well with your Internet Business!

On the other hand, if your sales letter's conversion rate is less than 1%, then you will need to take quick action to make your site sell more effectively. You may have to do more compelling copy writing, change the layout of your web pages or simply get a better and more attention-grabbing headline (which is so vital that it can make or break a sale!). Whatever you need to do, you have to increase your conversion rate from poor to excellent! To track visitors, you can subscribe to counter services if your web-hosting doesn't have a site statistic feature built in. To track sales, check your Credit Card Payment Processor.

How to Collect Payments

There are many online payment services which provide you with a simple way to accept payments. Unlike banks and credit card companies, services such as PayPal and ClickBank don't require a business to have a merchant account. They process the orders for you and the money is transferred to your bank account electronically.

Such services have become especially popular among those who use online auction sites (such as EBay), but many other online businesses are beginning to see the advantages of these services as well.

Although these services charge a small processing fee, it's less than you would normally pay for a credit card merchant account. Also, such services can be especially helpful when you need to arrange for small repetitive payments for hosting or an autoresponder.

But there are some drawbacks to using a payment service.

1. Many of them impose a daily or weekly limit on the amount of money that you send or receive. So if you want to exceed these limits you may find yourself incurring an additional fee for a "business account" or "premiere account".

2. These services are not banks, and therefore are not subject to strict banking regulations or protected by Federal Deposit Insurance.

3. Often these services provide their customers with less protection against fraud and abuse than many credit card companies offer.

4. Also, they are sometimes quick to freeze a customer's account if they suspect fraudulent or other criminal activities are taking place.

Before you sign up to any payment service, read their terms and conditions thoroughly. It is important that you fully understand and accept the service's dispute policy, limits on liability, their fee structure and any other rules or regulations that they may have.

It is also important that you do not keep too much money in your account, rather keep enough to conduct a few days of business and any unused funds should be transferred over to your regular bank account.

Following are a few more payment services that you may want to look at further when setting up an online business account.

1. Authorize.net. This service processes credit card and checking account transactions.

2. BidPay. This allows person to person payments. They accept a credit card payment from the payer and then send a money order to the payee.

3. BillPoint. This also allows person to person payments. Originally this system was being targeted specifically at EBay customers.

4. E-Gold. This allows the payment in gold (silver, platinum or palladium) to be made from one customer to another using an account based system.

5. PayPal. This is probably the most well-known payment service. It allows user to user payments and money transfers from funds in the user's PayPal account. It also allows payments by credit card and eCheck.

6. World Pay. This service provides both an internet merchant account, and payment processing service in one package.

CHAPTER 7- OTHER WAYS TO EARN MONEY FROM YOUR ONLINE BUSINESS

"What if I don't have what it takes to create my own product? What if I can't source for other people's product to sell?" "Can I still make my money from the Internet?" I heard you and the answer is a resounding YES. You can still have a business online even if you have NO products to sell. No one should question this possibility since people are doing this every day. "But how do they do that?" you wonder.

The Concept

Imagine you own your daily newspaper. How do you earn a lot of money from it? Selling them to your readers for a dollar or less each isn't going to profit you. So how are you going to profit from selling your daily newspaper? Selling advertisement spaces in your content? Precisely! Congratulate yourself if you've guessed the answer correctly. Give yourself a knock on the head if you have

Start Earning from Your Online Business

not! Okay, I was joking about that one but you can't be serious ALL the time, can you? Anyway, we'll move on with the subject.

Quite simply, the more people read your newspaper, the more money you can charge for your advertisements. The concept works the same for Internet Business. However, when you operate an Internet Business, you have the following advantages that you won't have if you run a conventional business:

- You don't have to invest a lot of money and effort into your Internet Business as opposed to conventional business.

- You don't need to deal with the delivery of your newspapers to reach to your readers on time every day.

- Publishing a newspaper is something that is beyond the reach of any individual together with the rewards that come with successful publication.

- The risk in conventional business is simply too high compared to Internet Business.

Sell Other People's Products

While there are several types of Internet Business Models to choose from to start, I would like to share with you some important gem information on how to start and run your online business as a reseller. Before we go any further, let us discuss whether this business is for you or not. This type of online business is for you if:

- You do not have your own product.

Page | 58

- You do not have what it takes to create a product from scratch as it demands a degree of talent, skill and expertise in any field.

- You just do not want to create your own product or simply do not have the time for it!

You will do well to consider this type of online business if you match one or more of the above statements. Now are you ready to find out how you can start your own resell rights business? If yes, then that is awesome. Read on!

What Is This Business Model All About?

Generally, you sell product(s) with resell rights and keep 100% of the profit. On top of that, the products you sold have affiliate links that can create back-end profits for you thus making residual income with no effort on your part.

What Is A Reseller?

A reseller buys a product, sells it and keeps 100% of the profits to him or herself. This is in contrary to being an affiliate whereby an affiliate sells other people's products for a commission.

What Are Resell Rights?

Resell rights allow one to resell the product and keep 100% of the profits with which without it, one is prohibited from selling the product to another person.

What Do You Need?

To start your online resell rights business, you will need to have a high-quality product with resell rights that can be customized. The product can be in the form of an E-book, software or even templates.

The first thing you should do is look for a product with resell rights to sell to your customers. When looking for one, you will want to take the following factors into consideration:

- Resell rights – the product must have resell rights in order for you to sell and keep 100% of the profits. If the product has no resell rights, you cannot use it for your reselling purpose.

- High in quality – a poor quality product will hardly make you any sale let alone back-end profits.

- Demand – are people seeking for information or solutions found in that product you are prospecting?

- Good sales letter and follow-up e-mails – if the principal's sales letter and follow-up e-mails do not persuade you to purchase his or her product then it is palpable that the result will be poor for you too as a reseller as you will also be using the principal's sales letter.

- Rare or uncommon – it pays to do a lot of research when starting your resell rights business. You must find out if the product is not over-saturated in the net market. If it is then your chances of selling the product are slim.

- Credibility and reputation – is the author a respected person? You can easily conduct a background check by typing his or her name in search engines and see the results.

- Back-end profits – find out how you can earn residual income without much effort on your part in the long run.

- Money-back guarantee – while I can actually omit this factor for it goes without saying most of the time, this is what you should look out for. High-quality products usually have 90-day money back guarantee. In case you discovered that the product is not for you or fail to make any sale in the first 90 days, you still have a chance to get your investment refunded.

Where Can You Find the Most Sellable Products?

Sourcing for the latest high-quality products with resell rights means doing some homework on your part. The best places to look for are:

- One-page Websites selling the latest product – you will want to pick the latest and hot product that there is a huge demand for, preferably not too old (1-2 years old).

- Active membership web sites dealing in giving products with resell rights – there are membership web sites that provide E-books and software with resell rights on a regular basis. You would know if the membership website contains the latest hot products by checking whether the webmaster sources for them often or not.

- Set-up Your Resell Rights Business. By now, I am going to assume that you have already picked a high-quality product with resell rights that you can customize it for back-end profits. This simply means purchasing the product yourself first. You will then work your business plan to cover your initial investment and later profit from it. The moment you get your hands on the product, what do you do? Read it! Use it! Remember I said that they are called products and not parcels? Sure, you do, if you have been reading up until now. I expect that since you are having a product with resell rights, it should also come with resell materials. Resell materials usually include:

• Web pages – Killer Sales Letter, Purchase Page, Thank You Page

• Images – your product (most important!), and miscellaneous

• Auto Responder letters – the e-mail follow ups you use for customers who opt into your follow-up mailing list. Since most of the job of selling the product and convincing your prospects is going to be done by your sales letter, you play your role very similar to a referrer or affiliate. Using ingenious concepts, you refer targeted prospects to your sales letter and if it is a good and persuasive sales letter, it can produce a conversion rate of 1 to 3%, hopefully more!

Marketing Your Product with all the technical issues taken care of, your web site ready and your product available for sale, you will need to promote your web site together with the product you are selling. Here are some effective ways you can practice for good results in your sales and back-end profits especially for this particular Internet Business Model:

• Create an Affiliate Income Opportunity – you can open an income opportunity to people who are interested in making money without having to create a product of their own through affiliate programs and directories. So long as you provide them a hefty commission of 50% to 75%, they would not mind selling on your behalf.

• You can establish a Joint Venture with E-zine Publishers as long as you provide them a chance to earn a percentage of your sales, say. 50 – 75%.

- You can comb the Internet for quality prospects. Membership web site owners and webmasters of your niche product are good targets. Send them a personal e-mail and get them to be interested in reviewing your product via the sales letter.

They will purchase your product for their own use or resell it and keep all the profits to themselves. What you are looking for is someone with great marketing power. As long as you have created a good back-end profit in the product, you will earn residual income more effectively by leveraging on other people's marketing power. This method is one of my favorites as most resellers actually do not bother to do the STP method – See Ten People a day.

- You can create a free report or E-book for viral marketing purposes and circulate it in your network. This is yet my other favorite. In the report or E-book, you provide free but useful information on a subject having to do with the product you are selling. Just be sure that it is not really a cloaked sales letter altogether. This will in turn, lead targeted prospects to your sales letter thus increasing your chances of making sales.

- Write articles having to do with the product you are selling. While you are not to write cloaked sales letters and submit them to article directories, giving free and beneficial information in your articles to people who are searching for it gives you credibility as you prove your worth. Again, this can result in targeted leads to your website and sales letter through your web site link in your resource box.

- Announce and promote the product in your mailing list. The bigger and higher quality your subscriber list is, the more sales you can make.

Start Earning from Your Online Business

- Create a website that channels to your product's sales letter – create web pages with content related to the product you are selling. The more relevant your web site is to your product, the more targeted your prospects are when you channel them to your sales letter through links and banner ads. This will improve your conversion rate as well.

While there are certainly more ways you can do to promote your website and drive targeted leads into your sales letter for good conversion rate of sales (let us not forget the back-end profits your product can also create!), most of these marketing plans can be followed easily with little to no cost on your part. Be aware that the reseller business is pretty tough competition.

You already win half the battle just by having the latest hot product to start with, more advantage if the product is not saturated yet. There you have it – what you need to start your very own resell rights business!

ABOUT THE AUTHOR

Karen Turner got an early start in the world of online marketing at the age of 19. She first started by selling items off her social media account then later on moved to creating a website, when her reputation as a seller was already established.

In 2012, Karen took the internet by storm when she started creating products and services that are targeted especially to internet marketers. Because these have been proven effective, she quickly rose to become an authority in the subject.

www.ingramcontent.com/pod-product-compliance
Lightning Source LLC
Chambersburg PA
CBHW051241170526
45165CB00004B/1524